Contents

Words that appear in the glossary are printed in **boldface** type the first time they occur in the text.

Modern-Day Wonders

Pick up your telephone. You can have a conversation with someone halfway around the world. Turn on your VCR and watch a TV program that aired last night after you went to bed. These are only some of the many wonders of **technology**.

Air travel is another amazing achievement of our modern world. How do airplanes fly? Let's find out.

4

Stuck on the Ground

Flying seems easy when we watch a gull gliding overhead. But a bird must overcome two forces in order to soar through the air.

Gravity pulls everything toward the ground. **Air resistance** slows anything moving through the air. For hundreds of years, people tried to overcome these natural forces. In the early 1900s, two brothers finally succeeded.

ASK ISAAC ASIMOV

HOW DO
AIRPLANES
FLY?

BY ISAAC ASIMOV AND ELIZABETH KAPLAN

Gareth Stevens Publishing
MILWAUKEE

For a free color catalog describing Gareth Stevens' list of high-quality children's books, call 1-800-341-3569 (USA) or 1-800-461-9120 (Canada).

Library of Congress Cataloging-in-Publication Data

Asimov, Isaac, 1920-
    How do airplanes fly? / by Isaac Asimov and Elizabeth Kaplan
        p. cm. — (Ask Isaac Asimov)
    Includes bibliographical references and index.
    Summary: Briefly describes how the forces of lift and thrust are used to overcome gravity and resistance to enable airplanes to fly.
    ISBN 0-8368-0800-2
    1. Flight—Juvenile literature. 2. Airplanes—Juvenile literature. [1. Flight. 2. Airplanes.] I. Kaplan, Elizabeth, 1956- . II. Title. III. Series: Asimov, Isaac, 1920- Ask Isaac Asimov.
    TL547.A79   1993
    629.13—dc20   92-27109

Edited, designed, and produced by
Gareth Stevens Publishing
1555 North RiverCenter Drive, Suite 201
Milwaukee, Wisconsin 53212, USA

Text © 1993 by Nightfall, Inc. and Martin H. Greenberg
End matter © 1993 by Gareth Stevens, Inc.
Format © 1993 by Gareth Stevens, Inc.

The book designer would like to thank Gift of Wings and the model for their cooperation.

Picture Credits
pp. 2-3, Courtesy of AMETEK, Inc.; pp. 4-5, © Picture Perfect USA; pp. 6-7, © Dick Poe/Visuals Unlimited; p. 6 (inset), © Mary Evans Picture Library; pp. 8-9, Courtesy of Special Collections and Archives, Wright State University; pp. 10-11, © Jon Allyn, Cr. Photog., 1992; pp. 12-13, Kurt Carloni/Artisan, 1992; pp. 14-15, © Adams Picture Library; pp. 16-17, Kurt Carloni/Artisan, 1992; pp. 18-19, © Joseph Giannetti/Third Coast Stock Source; pp. 20-21, Courtesy of NASA; pp. 22-23, Kurt Carloni/Artisan, 1992; p. 24, Kurt Carloni/Artisan, 1992

Cover photograph, © Mike Clarke/Adams Picture Library: A jumbo jet flies near St. Martin Airport in the Caribbean.

Series editor: Valerie Weber
Editors: Barbara J. Behm and Patricia Lantier-Sampon
Series designer: Sabine Beaupré
Book designer: Kristi Ludwig
Picture researcher: Diane Laska

Printed in the United States of America

1 2 3 4 5 6 7 8 9 98 97 96 95 94 93

The Wright Stuff

It was December 17, 1903, at Kitty Hawk,
North Carolina. Orville Wright stepped into
a gangly-looking machine, turned on the
motor, and climbed aloft into full flight.
With this first twelve-second ride, Orville
and Wilbur Wright made history.

The Wright brothers used two types of power to get their plane into the air. **Thrust** propelled the plane forward. **Lift** pulled it up into the air. Without these forces, no plane can fly. Orville and Wilbur Wright influenced world aviation for many years after Kitty Hawk. They built flying machines in the United States and Europe.

The Bernoulli Effect

The thrust of a plane's engine helps the plane achieve lift, which carries the plane into the air. These two forces make flight possible because of the **Bernoulli effect**.

Air flowing over a surface changes the **air pressure** on that surface. The faster the air flows, the lower the pressure. This is called the Bernoulli effect. You can see how this works if you blow over a strip of paper. The strip rises because pressure decreases over the paper as you blow.

Winging It

As a plane takes off, the Bernoulli effect becomes important. The diagrams show how the wings split the air into two streams. The curved shapes of the wings force the air to flow more quickly over the upper surface than under the lower surface. This decreases the air pressure on the upper surface because of the Bernoulli effect. So, the wings are lifted up by the greater pressure beneath the wings, carrying the plane into the air.

Air flowing over the wing splits into two streams.

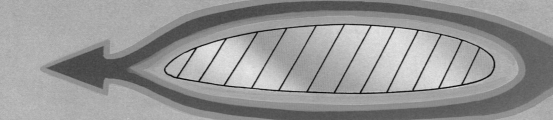

Air flowing over the wing covers a longer distance in the same amount of time as air flowing under the wing, so the air above the plane moves faster.

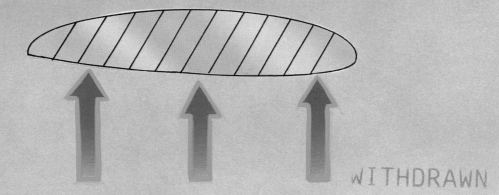

Because of the Bernoulli effect, pressure is greater below the wing than above it, so the wing rises.

Start Your Engines

A strong air current can lift a plane, but we can't always rely on wind power. A more reliable way to make air flow across the wings is to move the wings forward through the air. This is the job of the plane's engines.

A plane's engines drive the plane down the runway. Once in flight, the engines keep the plane moving through the air. Without this forward thrust, the plane would not be able to stay in the air.

15

Prop Plane, Jet Plane

Planes obtain thrust from either propellers or jet engines. The spinning propeller makes air move faster in front of the propeller than in back of it. This lowers the air pressure in front of the plane. The plane moves forward.

With a jet, air flows into the engine. The air is **compressed** and combined with fuel. A spark ignites the fuel and air mixture. The exploding gases escape from the back of the engine, thrusting the plane forward.

17

Inside the Cockpit

Flashing lights, spinning dials, buzzing buzzers — the **cockpit** whirs with activity as the pilot and copilot prepare for takeoff. They set switches and watch the instruments all around them. These instruments keep

18

track of the plane's speed, fuel, and many other things. The most important instruments are located right in front of the pilot. They map out the course the plane will take. With the aid of these instruments, the pilot can fly the plane safely to the desired destination.

Planes in Space

Some planes go up into space and **orbit** the Earth. The **space shuttle** is a combination spacecraft and airplane that is launched from a rocket. Astronauts use the shuttle to repair **satellites** and perform experiments. Then, they fly the shuttle back to Earth. The shuttle glides down through the clouds at high speeds. It needs an extra long runway to land safely. Then, the shuttle can be launched into space again.

20

Atlantis

The Future of Flight

Airplanes are so common that it's hard to believe they were once an impossible dream. But someday our jets may seem as old-fashioned as a horse and buggy. We may someday fly in sun-powered planes or hop into a miniplane to go to work. The future of flight is as limitless as the sky.

More Books to Read

Airplanes by Jeanne Bendick (Franklin Watts)
Airplanes by David Peterson (Childrens Press)
Finding Out About Things That Fly by Karen E. Little
    (EDC Publishing)
The Picture World of Airliners by R. J. Stephen (Franklin Watts)

Places to Write

Here are some places you can write for more information about the history of flight, airplanes, or the space shuttle. Be sure to tell them exactly what you want to know. Give them your full name and address so they can write back to you.

National Aviation Museum
National Museum of Science
    and Technology
Building 194
P.O. Box 9724
Ottawa Terminal
Ottawa, Ontario K1G 5A3

Wright Brothers National
    Memorial
Route 1, Box 675
Manteo, North Carolina 27954

National Air and Space Museum
Smithsonian Institution
Seventh Street and
    Independence Avenue SW
Washington, D.C. 20560

NASA Kennedy Space Center
Educational Services Office
Kennedy Space Center, Florida
    32899

Glossary

air pressure: the force that air exerts on anything it touches.

air resistance: the friction of air rubbing against anything that moves through it.

Bernoulli effect (bar-NOO-lee ih-FEKT): the decrease in air pressure that results when air movement increases.

cockpit: the cabin in a plane where the pilot and copilot sit.

compressed (cuhm-PREHST): forced to occupy a smaller space.

gravity (GRAV-uht-ee): the force that pulls everything toward Earth.

lift: the force that causes an airplane's wings to move upward.

orbit (AWR-buht): to circle a planet or star.

satellite (SAT-uhl-ite): an object or vehicle that circles any celestial body such as the Earth or the Moon. Satellites can receive and transmit television, radio, and other signals.

space shuttle: the reusable spacecraft that lands on a runway in the same way an airplane does.

technology (tehk-NAH-luh-jee): the use of scientific principles to produce things that are useful to people.

thrust: the force that causes a plane to move forward through the air.

Index